"My work is the embodiment of dreams in one form or another." - William Morris

RIGHT: Morris studied early woven textiles and the 'Peacock & Dragon' design was based on Sicilian silk weaves dating from the 15th and 16th century. In keeping with Morris' original version, this wool jacquard shown on the chair, was re-released in The Archive Collection of 2011, celebrating the 150th anniversary of Morris & Co. OPPOSITE: 'Kennet', designed by William Morris in 1883, was indigo discharged and block printed at Merton Abbey. PREVIOUS PAGE: 'Granada', this silk velvet, woven, printed and embellished with gilt thread, was designed and produced at Merton Abbey by William Morris in 1884, however, it proved so expensive that it was never commercially produced.

MORRIS & Co

First published in 2011 by Morris & Co.
Chalfont House, Oxford Road,
Denham, Buckinghamshire, UB9 4DX,
United Kingdom
www.william-morris.co.uk

ISBN 978-0-9568088-0-6

Designed by Jennifer Harmes
Styling by Jo Eaton

MORRIS & Co.
a revolution in decoration

Michael Parry

LEFT: The vine background in 'Peacock & Vine' is based on a block printed wallpaper designed by Morris in 1874. This was subsequently used by him in the creation of this 1879 crewelwork, to which peacock motifs were applied and attributed to Philip Webb.

MORRIS & Co. a revolution in decoration

Numerous books have been written about William Morris (1834-1896) and his resounding life, works and triumphs. This publication does not intend to duplicate history but rather to highlight the amazing accomplishments and successes achieved by, perhaps, the greatest of all the businesses in the Arts & Crafts Movement, co-founded, inspired and managed by Morris for 35 years. Its legacy is reflected by an astounding collection of unmistakeable wallpapers and fabrics on offer in the 21st century.

Interest in the remarkable talents of William Morris has never been greater than in recent years. He was a writer, poet, translator, publisher, fervent socialist, environmentalist and protector of ancient buildings as well as the most successful textile and wallpaper designer of his day. He pursued the age-old craft of block-printing wallpapers and fabrics, set up his own tapestry-weaving and hand-knotted carpet workshops and with his partners dominated stained-glass manufacture in Britain in the second half of the 19th century.

The authority that Morris & Co. brings to the marketplace is one of character, creative innovation and a style that – like much from the Victorian era – either appeals or repels. Today, the name Morris & Co. is synonymous with excellence of design, style, image, reliability and continuity founded on an aesthetic strategy conceived 150 years ago, yet whose images have been successively re-interpreted for today with tomorrow in mind.

From clutter to clarity

William Morris was three years old when Queen Victoria came to the throne in 1837. At that time, upper-middle class domestic interiors were dominated by the French Rococo style. These cluttered Victorian interiors persisted throughout the century with swathes of velvet, innumerable pieces of furniture and collections of photographs and souvenirs littering every available surface.

Vast fortunes were being made in commerce and banking; the *nouveaux riche* spending huge sums making their homes opulent and pseudo-French whilst the upper classes remained true to their silk brocades and hand block printed wallpapers. The Industrial Revolution and the steam-powered mass production it spawned changed everything. Hand block printed wallpapers were challenged by new surface roller printed wallpapers from machines first patented in 1839 and by the late 1800s these mass produced papers had become more dominant.

Attitudes to home decoration in the mid-19th century were somewhat different from those of today. Numerous works were published on household management, cookery and etiquette, yet there was little guidance on how to decorate and furnish your home. For advice on interior decoration the householder was at the mercy of the upholsterer, whose prime objective was to persuade customers to spend as much as possible.

It was only towards the end of the 19th century that home decorating became a popular pastime. Publications on household management featured numerous articles by notable designers, including William Morris.

One of the key developments of the period was the emergence of department stores; the most prominent, Bainbridges Newcastle (now John Lewis), Derry & Toms, Swan & Edgar and Liberty of London, heralding a new era

for interior decoration where merchandise was branded, identified and priced. This innovative retail strategy enabled married couples to furnish their homes with the help and impartial advice of the stores' sales assistants.

Another major domestic influence was the advent of electric light in 1878, which exposed the grime and dust within Victorian interiors. This led to a growing awareness of hygiene and a tendency to buy machine-printed fabrics and wallpapers, as these were relatively inexpensive and easy to replace. However, ornamentation persisted, even on walls, which were divided into three sections, dado, filling and frieze, each decorated with a separate wallpaper.

It was William Morris and the Arts & Crafts and Aesthetic Movements that trail-blazed simplicity, craftsmanship and design inspired by nature.

A revolution in decoration

William Morris' career as a designer emerged in 1861, triggered by two key events – decorating the Oxford Union in 1857 and building Red House in Bexleyheath with the architect Philip Webb.

Morris and Webb became friends in 1856 when both were working for the Gothic revival architect, George Edmund Street. On his marriage to Jane Burden in 1859, Morris built his first home, Red House, designed by Webb. Appalled by the over-elaborate products and furnishings available at the time, Morris and his friends decorated Red House in the medieval style, creating furnishings, embroideries, stained-glass windows, ceiling and mural decorations, tapestries and textiles.

On completion of the interior in 1861 Morris and his comrades decided to turn their domestic hobby into a commercial enterprise by creating medieval-inspired handcrafted items for the home. The venture would ultimately lead Morris to revolutionise public attitudes towards decorative arts and interior decoration in particular.

William Morris

Edward Burne-Jones

Dante Gabriel Rossetti

The Firm – A creative collective

Morris, Marshall, Faulkner & Company, colloquially known as 'The Firm', was established in 1861, initially more as a society of friends united by a common purpose and youthful idealism than as a business partnership. The founding members were William Morris, the painters Ford Madox Brown (1821-1893), Dante Gabriel Rossetti (1828-1882) and Edward Burne-Jones (1833-1898), Peter Paul Marshall (1830-1900), an engineer and amateur artist, the architect Philip Webb (1831-1915), and Charles James Faulkner (1833-1892), a mathematician, Oxford don and, in the early years, the company's book keeper. They set up a studio at 8 Red Lion Square in Bloomsbury, London.

The objective was for each partner to create designs for decorative products. This they did in varying degrees, with the exception of Faulkner, although his sisters, Kate and Lucy, both later designed for the company. The partners' remuneration would probably have been based on the number of individual commissions and revenues each partner contributed, before the profits of the company were divided equally among the members.

Initially, the group's practical expertise was quite limited and the making of products tended to be outsourced to others, only to be brought in-house as the various techniques were mastered and the workshops were expanded or relocated. This applied to most products including stained glass, furniture, tapestries and fabrics, the exception being wallpaper printing.

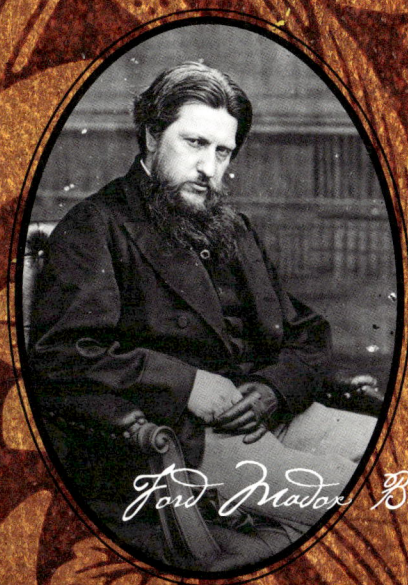

Ford Madox Brown

Philip Webb

Charles Faulkner

The luxury of taste

Morris' philosophy was that good quality furnishings should be available to all and not just the wealthy. Regrettably, his aims were at odds with each other, as handcrafted goods were far more expensive than machine-made alternatives. Nonetheless, his mission was to emphasise the 'Luxury of Taste' rather than the 'Luxury of Costliness'.

The partners marketed 'The Firm' as manufacturers of inexpensive, handmade artistic products. Their strategy to offer quality at a price was judged by their competitors to be foolhardy and considered by others as far from conventional.

OPPOSITE: 'Vine' was designed by William Morris in 1873 and was later printed on a metallic and lacquered embossed paper first seen in 1875.
THIS PAGE: Between 1877 and 1878, Morris created the original 'Sunflower' watercolour design in classic 'mirror repeat'. This 1881 version was block printed in red oil on a crepe-embossed, foiled and lacquered ground.

THIS PAGE: 'The Adoration of the Magi', commissioned in 1887 by John Prideaux Lightfoot, Rector of Exeter College, Oxford, for the chapel. Both William Morris and Edward Burne-Jones worked on the tapestry together with John Henry Dearle who provided added background detail typified by his characteristic stylised flora. The tapestry was finally completed at the Morris & Co. workshop at Merton Abbey in 1902.

RIGHT: 'Adam Naming the Animals' forms part of the 'Creation' window at All Saints Church in Selsley, Gloucestershire. Designed by Philip Webb and William Morris, it was the first stained glass set produced by Morris, Marshall, Faulkner & Co., circa 1862.

Gothic revival & ecclesiastical decoration

Church decoration was central to 'The Firm' from the beginning. Apart from aesthetic reasons for starting the business, the cult of medievalism from the mid to late 19th century led to significant turnover from the mushrooming of new-build churches and the major refurbishment of old churches.

By the 1860s the demand for Gothic Revival bestowed success on the business due to Morris and Webb's associations with the architectural world and commissions from George Edmund Street and George F. Bodley for ecclesiastical stained glass and church furnishings.

Initially, 'The Firm' concentrated on stained glass predominantly designed by Edward Burne-Jones, followed by church decoration, carving, metalwork, mural decorations and furniture. At the International Exhibition in London in 1862, Morris, Marshall, Faulkner & Co. received awards for stained glass, decorated furniture and embroideries (referred to at the time as tapestries). It was probably here that Bodley confirmed his commission for the stained-glass windows at All Saints

Church in Selsley, Gloucestershire. Perhaps the most complete Morris church is St Martin's in Brampton, Cumbria, being the only church designed by Philip Webb and containing one of the most exquisite sets of stained-glass windows designed by Burne-Jones and made in the Morris & Co. workshops.

'The Firm' also created jewellery, glass, tiles, carpets and embroideries, the latter being one of the mainstays of the business. It was at Oxford in 1857 that William Morris hand-stitched his first embroidery with his philosophy, 'Si je puis' (If I can). Consequently he designed two further embroidery patterns, Daisy and Sunflower, the catalyst for the rich yet delicate, hand-stitched ecclesiastical furnishings for which Morris, Marshall, Faulkner & Co. became recognised.

In 1865, 'The Firm' moved to 26 Queen Square, Bloomsbury, London. Two years later they were commissioned to decorate the Green Dining Room at the South Kensington Museum (now known as the Victoria and Albert Museum) and the Armoury and Tapestry Rooms at St James' Palace. These commissions were the turning point in the firm's popularity.

Lily colouring. green ground

Hyacinths, the redder blue.
Wood sorrel, the outline a little stronger than in drawing. but not too brown keep it pinky in shade.
Lilies copy as nearly as you can
Chrysanthemum, the tint of the right hand flower, the seeds are the same colour as the stamens of Lily

Leaves

In wood sorrel leaves there are two shades of green, the stalks & outlines being one. Use the two darker shades for leaves of Hyacinth. (get new block cut for these leaves) Leaves of Lily have 2 tints of green rather colder than those of Hyacinth leaves. Make leaves of Chrysanthemum of the darker shade of lily leaves. not too colours.

Hyacinth stalks to print B
Hyacinth leaves & go into A
Veins of Hyacinth Leaves to be same as outline of Sorrel

THIS PAGE: This original trial sample of 'Lily' wallpaper, designed by William Morris in 1874, was returned by him to Jeffrey & Co. with a note advising colour changes. RIGHT: One of two stand books contained within the Morris & Co. Archive displaying block printed and a few machine printed wallpapers.

Think first of the walls

Morris attempted to print wallpaper within a year of founding 'The Firm'. For *Trellis*, his first design, his intention to use zinc plates replicating wash tints similar to those achieved by print engraving was not practical. Therefore he sought the services of Barrett's of Bethnal Green to hand-cut traditional pear-wood printing blocks. These were used from 1864 by Jeffrey & Company, who provided a separate block-printing department solely for Morris & Co. wallpapers.

It was always Morris' intention to design wallpapers within the constraints of manufacturing rather than creating one-off 'wall paintings'. Of all his products of domestic ornamentation the 'wallpaper hangings' became the most widely popular.

In the late 1860s Morris concentrated his decorative prowess on wallpaper and textile designs. His first three repeating wallpaper patterns were most famously *Trellis*, *Daisy* and *Fruit*; their popularity, enduring appeal and success continue to this day. *Trellis* was inspired by the trellis work and rose garden at Red House, with birds drawn by Philip Webb. *Daisy* and *Fruit*, probably inspired by naïve medieval wood cut illustrations, are less sophisticated than designs such as *Acanthus* (1875) which uses the complex layering technique for which Morris became famous.

Morris & Co. issued more than 100 block printed wallpaper patterns, of which William Morris designed over half, the balance being designed by John Henry Dearle (33), Kate Faulkner (4), May Morris (3), Kathleen Kersey (2), George Gilbert Scott Jnr (1 adapted), W.A.S. Benson (1-2), with three adapted and seven unattributed. This output was considered to be relatively insignificant compared to rival businesses, yet these wallpapers continue to influence interior decoration throughout the world.

Whatever you have in your rooms think first of the walls; for they are that which makes your house and home; and if you don't make some sacrifice in their favour, you will find your chambers have a kind of makeshift, lodging-house look about them, however rich and handsome your movables may be. – William Morris

12

THIS PAGE: Wallpaper is perhaps the most celebrated of all William Morris' works having designed 46 wallpapers and five ceiling papers. Jeffrey & Company printed all his block printed papers under the personal supervision of their managing director, Metford Warner. Morris closely monitored all production processes paying close attention, not only to design interpretation, but also the colouration of each and every pattern. OPPOSITE: First registered in 1876, the original design for 'Pimpernel' wallpaper was created by William Morris and decorated the dining room walls of his London home, Kelmscott House. The wallpaper shown is from The Archive Collection of 2011.

"All rooms ought to look as if they were lived in, and to have, so to say, a friendly welcom ready for the incomer." - William Morris

Block-printed textiles

In 1868 William Morris approached Bannister Hall Print Works to produce 'The Firm's' first block-printed fabrics. These were reproductions of mid-1830s chintzes, now considered at odds with the inimitable Morris style, but at the time proved popular. The first fabric Morris designed was *Jasmine Trellis*, circa 1870, which bears a resemblance to his *Trellis* wallpaper, however, he preferred his second pattern, *Tulip & Willow*, circa 1873, which was subsequently indigo-discharge-printed at the workshop at Merton Abbey – an old technique reintroduced by Morris.

Morris began to experiment with vegetable and other natural dyes for fabric printing in conjunction with Thomas Wardle at Leek in Staffordshire, using kermes, cochineal, indigo, yellow from weld, blue from woad and red from the madder plant, to name but a few. He considered modern aniline chemical dyes 'hideous' and 'cheap and nasty', the outcome being, 'Foul blotches of the capitalist dyer', whereas 'old dyes fade naturally'. By 1878 he had outsourced the fabric printing to Wardle.

OPPOSITE: In 1873 William Morris designed 'Tulip & Willow', his second textile design, initially printed by Thomas Clarkson of Bannister Hall. Appalled by the result, Morris eventually successfully discharged and block printed this design using indigo blue at the Merton Abbey workshop in 1883. LEFT INSET: Morris' goal to revive age-old recipes and skills using natural plant, vegetable and animal dyestuffs was realised at Merton Abbey. They were used by Morris to dye wool yarns, seen here, prior to tapestry weaving. THIS PAGE: 'Large Stem', the earliest Morris & Co. fabric, was a series of adapted 1830s Bannister Hall chintzes, which Morris then block printed in the late 1860s to the early 1870s.

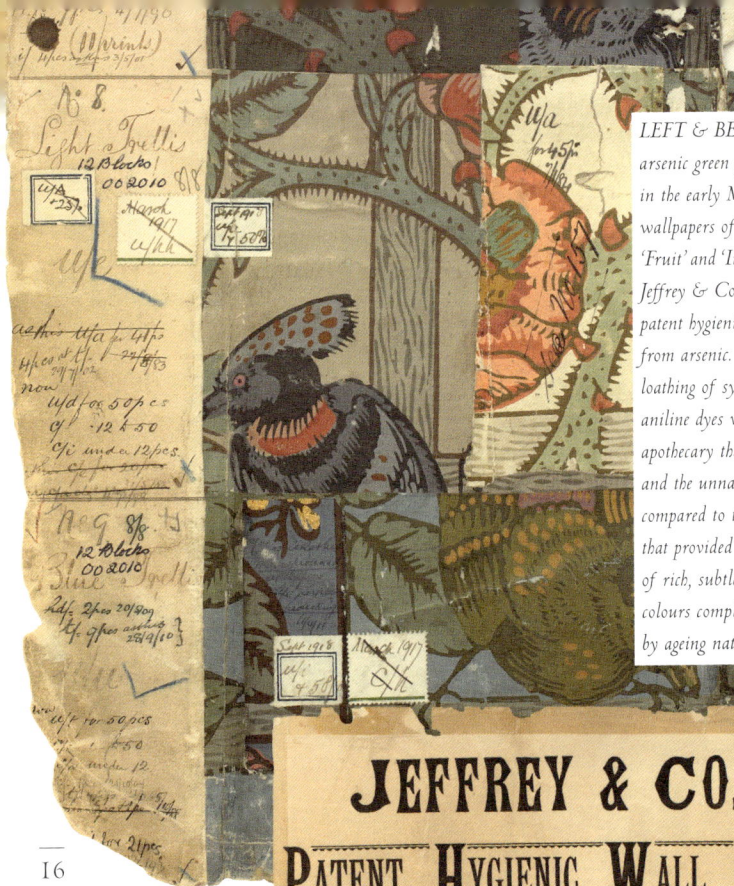

LEFT & BELOW: Although arsenic green pigment was used in the early Morris & Co. wallpapers of 'Trellis', 'Daisy', 'Fruit' and 'Indian', by the 1870s Jeffrey & Co. had opted to launch patent hygienic wallpapers free from arsenic. RIGHT: Morris' loathing of synthetic, chemical, aniline dyes was founded on the apothecary theory, the garish results and the unnatural fading qualities compared to those of natural dyes that provided him with a variety of rich, subtle and harmonious colours complementing each other by ageing naturally.

JEFFREY & CO.'S PATENT HYGIENIC WALL PAPERS

Are free from Arsenic,

And may be cleaned by Sponging with Soap and Water without disturbing the Colors.

PAPERS prepared with J. & Co.'s Patent are coated with an impervious solution which renders them non-absorbent and at the same time prevents any particles of colour or dust becoming detached from the surface; thus forming a perfectly SANITARY PAPER. They will be found very useful Bedrooms, Nurseries and on Staircases, as they can cleaned with Soap and Water when required.

Papers (free from Arsenic) but not rendered Washable are supplied at lower price.

The two prices are marked on the back of each pattern.

Factory: 64 ESSEX ROAD, ISLINGTON, N.

The dangers of colour

Whilst the resplendence of wallpapers brightened up many Victorian homes, their colours hid demonic ingredients. Many children were overwhelmed and killed by fumes in bedrooms papered with materials containing arsenic green and other toxic elements. Their dangers were periodically reported in 1860s London newspapers, which alleged that 'the atmosphere of dwellings all over Britain was more or less poisoned with arsenic'. Nonetheless, they continued to be used until the 1880s.

Arsenic production also contributed to William Morris' private means. In 1855, when he came of age, he inherited a substantial annual income. Some £700 of it (equivalent to £50,000 today) was generated by share-dividends from the southwest England copper and arsenic mining company, Devon Great Consols, which produced around half of the entire British output of refined arsenic. Morris was a part-time director of the company for a number of years and only sold his shares in the late 1870s.

Recent evidence verifies that early Morris & Co. wallpapers contained poisonous ingredients since Morris rejected synthetic new 'chemical' dyes in favour of more customary mineral pigments. The unguarded dangers masquerading within *Trellis*, *Daisy* and *Fruit* wallpapers did not deter sales to affluent patrons; moreover, *Trellis* decorated the corridors and bedrooms of Morris' own homes of Red House and Kelmscott Manor.

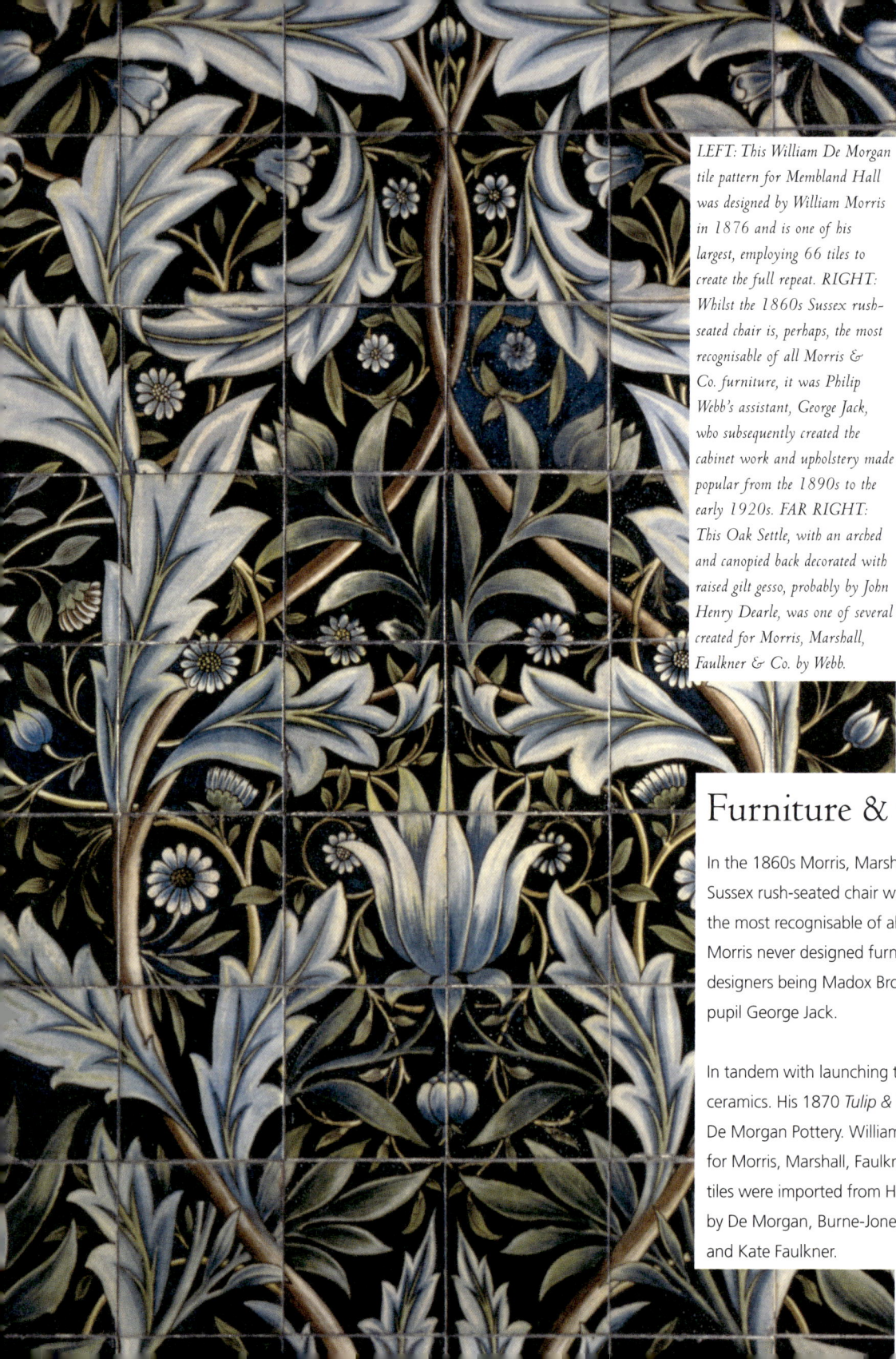

LEFT: This William De Morgan tile pattern for Membland Hall was designed by William Morris in 1876 and is one of his largest, employing 66 tiles to create the full repeat. RIGHT: Whilst the 1860s Sussex rush-seated chair is, perhaps, the most recognisable of all Morris & Co. furniture, it was Philip Webb's assistant, George Jack, who subsequently created the cabinet work and upholstery made popular from the 1890s to the early 1920s. FAR RIGHT: This Oak Settle, with an arched and canopied back decorated with raised gilt gesso, probably by John Henry Dearle, was one of several created for Morris, Marshall, Faulkner & Co. by Webb.

Furniture & tiles

In the 1860s Morris, Marshall, Faulkner & Co. introduced the Sussex rush-seated chair with an ebonised frame which became the most recognisable of all Morris & Co. furniture. William Morris never designed furniture, 'The Firm's' key furniture designers being Madox Brown, Rossetti, Webb and later Webb's pupil George Jack.

In tandem with launching textiles, Morris expanded into ceramics. His 1870 *Tulip & Trellis* tile was manufactured by the De Morgan Pottery. William Frend De Morgan initially worked for Morris, Marshall, Faulkner & Co. in the 1860s when white tiles were imported from Holland to be hand-tinted and painted by De Morgan, Burne-Jones, Morris, Madox Brown, Rossetti and Kate Faulkner.

THE SUSSEX RUSH-SEATED CHAIRS

MORRIS AND COMPANY
449 OXFORD STREET, LONDON, W.

OMPANY
ED

NO. 102. LADDER-BACK SINGLE
IN GREEN OR BROWN STAIN, £4

"ROSSETTI" ARM-CHAIR.
IN BLACK, 16/6.

SUSSEX CORNER CHAIR.
IN BLACK, 11/6.

SUSSEX SINGLE CHAIR,
IN BLACK, 7/-.

SUSSEX ARM-CHAIR,
IN BLACK, 9/9.

NO. 150. ARM-CHAIR,
IN GREEN OR BROWN STAIN, 19/6.

SUSSEX SINGLE CHAIR.
IN BLACK, 10/6.

SUSSEX SETTEE, FEET. 5IN. LONG.
IN BLACK, 35/-.

ROUND SEAT PIANO CHAIR.
IN BLACK, 10/6.

"Of all the specific minor improvements in common household objects due to Morris, the rush-bottomed Sussex chair perhaps takes the first place. It was not his own invention, but was copied with trifling improvements from an old chair of village manufacture picked up in Sussex. With or without modification it has been taken up by all the modern furniture manufacturers, and is in almost universal use. But the Morris pattern of the later type (there were two) still excels all others in simplicity and elegance of proportion."

"Life of William Morris": By J. W. Mackail.

63

"I should say that the making of ugly pottery was one of the most remarkable inventions of our civilisation."

— William Morris

MORRIS

WALL-PAPERS

BY

MORRIS & COMPANY Ltd.

449 OXFORD STREET,

LONDON, W.

AND MERTON ABBEY, SURREY.

DECORATION

LEFT: 'Acanthus' was designed by William Morris in 1874, being the first of a series of grand-scale wallpapers reflecting the instantly recognisable layering of foliage and requiring 30 blocks to print the full repeat; seen in all its glory in The Acanthus Bedroom at Wightwick Manor. OPPOSITE: Morris & Co. issued several price lists to promote its goods and services including 'Wall-Papers' shown here dating from 1907.

Morris & Co.

By 1874 it was apparent that the principles, beliefs, viewpoints and convictions of the partners were somewhat at odds with each other due to the inequality of profit share and imbalance of workloads, Morris having the misfortune of being the greatest loser.

In 1875, after much legal unpleasantness, Morris dissolved Morris, Marshall, Faulkner & Co. by removing his inactive partners and settling their considerable liabilities – buying them out. The same year he re-launched Morris & Co., with himself as sole proprietor. The character of the business remained unchanged.

On the birth of Morris & Co., Burne-Jones became the principal designer creating hundreds of cartoons for stained-glass windows and this, coupled with the already considerable contribution made by Madox Brown, resulted in Morris & Co. dominating English stained-glass manufacture throughout the 1870s and 1880s.

This period proved to be the busiest and most creative of William Morris' life.

Decorators of the moment

While William Morris took inspiration from traditional crafts, his commercial acumen was forward thinking. He was aware not only of the market place, but also of the needs and demands of consumers. His perspicacity and prudence for improving standards of interior decoration culminated in his opening a shop, showroom and business premises at 449, Oxford Street in 1877. The strategy was to sell interior products for the whole home, not only by Morris & Co., but also ceramics by William De Morgan, metalwork by W.A.S. Benson and glass by James Powell. This undertaking was no idle whim, but a considered business venture where design, manufacturing, marketing and sales interlocked to generate profits.

The first significant accolade was bestowed on Morris at the 1862 International Exhibition in London. Equally effective for credibility and sales was Charles L. Eastlake's influential 1868 book, *Hints on Household Taste in Furniture, Upholstery and Other Details*. In Chapter four, *The Floor and the Wall*, he states: '*Messrs. Morris, Marshall, [sic Faulkner] & Company, of Queen Square, Bloomsbury, have produced some admirable examples [of paper hangings].*'

The development of new markets and greater brand awareness necessitated the appointment of sales agents for Morris & Co. in the United States, Australia and Europe in the 1880s. Punitive import duties plagued William Morris, but his determination to export interior products to some extent succeeded because wealthy international clients were prepared to pay exorbitant prices for superlative merchandise bearing the Morris & Co. brand.

Throughout the 1880s, Morris & Co. commanded respect and admiration for the quality of its stained glass, furniture, rugs, carpets, tapestries, embroideries, wallpapers, chintzes, cotton prints, wall hangings, brocades and damasks, all of which were showcased on an impressive scale. Morris and Burne-Jones marketed themselves as decorators of the moment and were much in demand. Moreover, through Philip Webb's domestic architecture, wealthy homeowners such as the Ionides of Holland Park and the Beales of Standen were recommended to Morris & Co. for a complete interior decorating service.

LEFT: This stand book contained within the Morris & Co. Archive was last seen on display in the Morris & Co. Showroom at 17 George Street, Hanover Square, London, during the late 1930s.

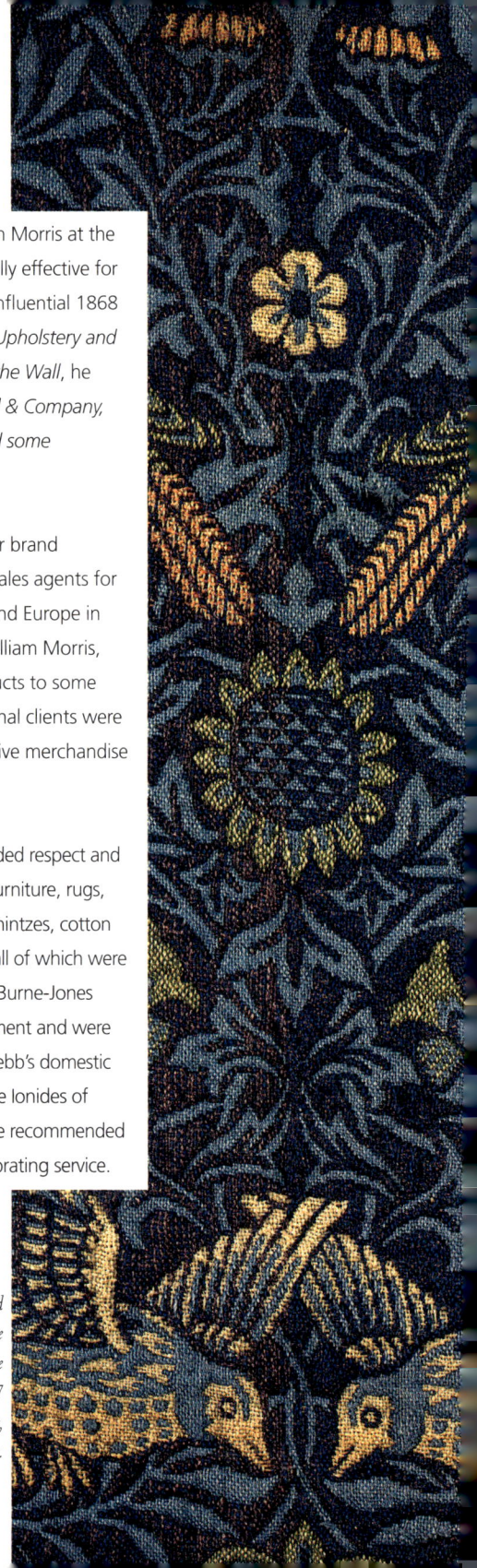

*THIS PAGE: 'Bird',
designed by William Morris
in 1877 and illustrated
in a 1907 Morris & Co.
catalogue as 'The Bird' hand
woven tapestry in madder
red or indigo blue colouring.
ABOVE: The 449 Oxford
Street, London premises was
not only an emporium of arts
& crafts merchandise but also
the headquarters of Morris
& Co. attracting an affluent
clientele to the 'Decorators
of the moment'.*

THIS PAGE: *The original carpet, 'Bullerswood', was designed by William Morris and John Henry Dearle and woven at Merton Abbey in 1889 being one specially created for Bullerswood, a house in Kent. This fine example of 'Hammersmith' carpets was heavily influenced by Morris' interest in Persian carpets and Islamic art. RIGHT: Morris seldom designed tapestries, yet 'The Woodpecker', his first, designed circa 1885, incorporated poetry and became the blueprint for many to follow, Edward Burne-Jones and John Henry Dearle became the key designers.*

Woven textiles, carpets & tapestry weaving

In 1877 Morris produced his first woven textiles at a newly rented workshop in Great Ormond Yard, adjacent to 26 Queen Square. Weaving was his last decorative opus and caused him much heartache in bringing together the aesthetic, theoretical, technical and practical elements essential to the creation of a perfect weave.

Morris agonised and experimented with the revival of old manufacturing techniques that he felt had been destroyed by the advent of the Industrial Revolution, yet his blueprint for utilising medieval techniques to create wondrous products for the common people never became a reality despite his much talked about belief in 'art for all'. Instead, Morris & Co. catered for the fashionable wealthy elite, an enigma that would follow Morris to his grave.

Towards the end of the 1870s, Morris, with thoughts of resurrecting the Mortlake tapestry weaving that had been closed down in 1703, embarked on trials with tapestries and carpets exploiting hand-knotting techniques similar to those of the Flemish 'Arras' tapestry weavers. Within two years he had set up looms in the Coach House adjoining his Hammersmith home.

Handmade 'Hammersmith' carpets and rugs, as they became known, were unquestionably expensive but their cost was offset by sub-contracted Wilton, Axminster, Brussels and Kidderminster carpets at what were considered reasonable prices, specifically aimed at the new middle-class. The 'Hammersmith' trademark was used by Morris to differentiate his exclusive hand-knotted rugs from his outsourced machine-woven carpets.

"Ornamental pattern work, to be raised above the contempt of reasonable men, must possess three qualities: beauty, imagination and order." - William Morris

THIS PAGE: In excess of 60 tapestries, damasks, brocades, figured silks and velvets were created and woven at Merton Abbey, providing an invaluable source of inspiration for designs contained within The Archive Collections of 2011, celebrating the 150th anniversary of Morris & Co. OPPOSITE: 'Fruit Embroidery' from the 2007 Embroideries Collection. Having taught himself embroidery, William Morris was key to the development of ecclesiastical embroidery for which 'The Firm' would become famous.

Literary & political pursuits

Morris' interests frequently extended beyond 'The Firm'. In the late 1860s he created *The Earthly Paradise*, a huge collection of poems. Unleashing his backlash against the Industrial Revolution, he wrote:

'Forget six Counties overhung with smoke.
Forget the snorting steam and piston stroke.
Forget the spreading of the hideous town.
Think rather of a packhorse on the down!'

During the 1870s politics diverted Morris' attention away from his business and in 1877, with Philip Webb, founded the Society for the Protection of Ancient Buildings (SPAB), Britain's oldest conservation body. By the early 1880s he had converted to socialism, vigorously opposing poverty, unemployment and the growing gap between the upper and lower classes. He banded together with his supporters to form The Socialist League and remained an active member for some ten years. By 1890 he had withdrawn from the league but retained his position generally in the socialist movement.

The desire for his own printing press became his new preoccupation, provoked by vehement dissatisfaction with book design of the time. This ambition was eventually fulfilled in 1891 when the Kelmscott Press was established.

The collaboration between Morris and Burne-Jones created some of the finest books since medieval times, including the *Kelmscott Chaucer*, with engravings by Burne-Jones. The Kelmscott Press at Hammersmith was the most famous of all the private presses of the Arts & Crafts Movement, producing more than 50 works. It remained in operation until 1898, following the deaths of both Morris and Burne-Jones.

28

ABOVE: The Kelmscott Press was the lifelong fulfilment of Morris' interest in book design inspired by medieval books where text was hand written and illustrations printed by woodcut. His renowned 'News from Nowhere' issued in 1893 is, perhaps, the finest book created since medieval times.
RIGHT: Morris used two typefaces, one early Venetian and the other early German, stamping them with decorative borders and ink printing on handmade paper.

...OWHERE OR...
...EST.
...USSION AND

...P at the League,
...says a friend, there
...had been one night
...a brisk conversa-
...tional discussion,
...as to what would
happen on the
Morrow of the Re-
volution, finally
...rous statement by
...views on the future
...new society.
...r friend: Consider-
...subject, the discus-
...s good-tempered;
...present, being used
...meetings & after-
...debates, if they did
...'s opinions, which
...ted of them, at all
...attempt to speak
...stom of people in
...when conversing

William Morris and May Morris with the staff at Kelmscott Press

William Morris with the Socialist League

In 1881 William Morris moved his company's workshops to Merton Abbey. Since the mid 1700s the site had hosted calico printing due to its location on the River Wandle, supplying water essential to the preparation, printing and finishing of cretonnes and chintzes. With conservation in mind, Morris refused to alter the existing buildings in any way but customised them to meet his manufacturing needs. The buildings remained virtually intact until the company closed down in 1940. Yet by the early 1950s war damage, housing redevelopment and commercial expansion ravaged this famous site. Today, Merton Abbey is once again the subject of the conservation that was so dear to Morris' heart.

Merton Abbey

With Morris & Co. offering a complete decoration service, it was necessary to relocate to bigger workshops. In 1881 land and property was acquired at Merton Abbey in south-west London. The site on the River Wandle was chosen for its plentiful supply of water, essential for the dyeing and printing of textiles. In the same year, Queen Square closed and all remaining commercial affairs transferred to Oxford Street.

The existing Merton Abbey buildings were customised for the creation of artisan crafts, including vat dyeing and block-printing cretonnes and chintzes, hand-knotting and weaving carpets and tapestries, weaving damasks and brocades in both silk and wool, and, of course, drawing artwork, cutting, hand-colouring, kiln-firing and lead setting of stained glass.

Merton Abbey provided the space needed to accommodate the large, high-warp 'Arras-type' tapestry looms. Morris longed to create medieval-style tapestries and, once again, sought inspiration and guidance from the past to assist him in the construction of looms similar to those of the medieval Flemish weavers.

By contrast, Morris and Burne-Jones made good use of Frederick Hollyer's sophisticated, state-of-the-art photography in the production of stained glass, tapestries and books.

The mid 1880s saw Morris & Co. wares at their most popular. More than 20 wallpaper patterns were created, including *Bird & Anemone* (1882), *Honeysuckle* (1883) and *Willow Bough* (1887). However, by the end of the decade William Morris was showing less interest in the Merton Abbey workshops, passing them over to his assistant, John Henry Dearle, to manage on his behalf.

John Henry Dearle's career can solely be attributed to the influence of his employer and mentor, William Morris, although following Morris' death, Dearle rarely received credit for his creative prowess. Yet he upheld Morris' inspirational legacy by creating innovative products based on vintage crafts, flawless materials, virtuous work ethics and accomplished designs based on Morris' principles.

John Henry Dearle (1860-1932)

John Henry Dearle was first employed in 1878 by Morris & Co. as a teenage assistant in the Oxford Street shop prior to working as a trainee in the stained-glass studio in Queen Square. Morris, accompanied by his young protégé – at that time Dearle was his tapestry assistant – set up a loom in Great Ormond Yard and by the early 1880s Dearle was responsible for training the tapestry assistants. His natural aptitude for design culminated in his creation of repeating wallpaper and textile patterns in the Morris style, his first being *Iris* wallpaper in 1887.

Morris, his daughter May, and Dearle were the key designers of embroidery patterns for fire screens, folding screens, cushion covers, table linen, wall hangings and portière door curtains. These were sold either as completed works or, for the more ambitious, as embroidery kits at various levels of completion. In 1885, Dearle developed four-fold mahogany screens that sold for £4.10 shillings, covered in either embroidery patterns or exclusive designs of imported Japanese embossed leather papers. From then until 1900, Dearle designed embroidery panels under the directorship of May Morris.

In 1881, Dearle took control of tapestry weaving at Merton Abbey, becoming art director in 1896, the year of Morris' death. He was responsible for interior design commissions and managing the studios and works at Merton Abbey until his death in 1932, having worked at Morris & Co. for a total of 54 years.

THIS PAGE: A magnificent jacquard woven interpretation of 'Artichoke', block printed wallpaper, designed by John Henry Dearle between 1898 and 1899, without doubt one of Dearle's most sensational designs. OPPOSITE: 'Golden Lily' (left) and 'Artichoke' (right). The iconic Morris & Co. design 'Golden Lily', frequently attributed to William Morris, was also designed by Dearle in 1899 and is now reissued as a surflex wallpaper in The Archive Collections of 2011.

The death of William Morris

William Morris died on the 3rd October 1896 aged 62 and lies beneath a simple Philip Webb tombstone in St George's Churchyard in Kelmscott, Oxfordshire. In his will, taken from a press cutting at that time, he states:

'I expressly empower my trustees to realise or postpone the realisation of my interest in the business of Morris & Co. I further authorise my trustees, either jointly or concurrently with the partners or surviving partner therein to sell the said business by private contract, tender or auction.'

After Morris' death, the metal worker William (W.A.S.) Benson, a friend of both Morris & Burne-Jones, became chairman of Morris & Co. supported by the controlling hands of Morris' junior partners, the brothers Frank and Robert Smith (appointed business managers 19 years earlier), with John Henry Dearle managing the studios at Merton Abbey.

As Morris' successor, Dearle was responsible for creating designs almost indistinguishable from his mentor, for which he had natural capability and creative dexterity; his products were frequently sold under the Morris & Co. name.

The business, under the new management and suffering from the loss of their founder and guardian, was in desperate need of strategic direction and languished at this time. This was then compounded by the death of Sir Edward Burne-Jones in 1898, at the age of 65, leaving all creative and artistic responsibilities to Dearle.

In 1905 the company was sold to Henry Currie Marillier (a former partner in W.A.S. Benson's metal works) and re-registered as Morris & Co. Decorators Ltd. With the exception of Dearle, the board consisted of businessmen with little or no artistic flair. Consequently the company's character changed, and it became a copycat firm competing for the Edwardian market and desperately trying to hold on to its Morris heredity.

Slowly and progressively the Morris business regained some of its lost reputation and credibility most notably through the adaptation of earlier block-printed wallpapers into printed cottons and linens, together with a decision that would have incurred Morris' wrath, namely the manufacture of five wallpaper designs printed on surface roller machines using water-based emulsions.

The five designs were *Carnation*, *Merton* (both by Kate Faulkner, 1880 and 1888), *Oak Tree*, *Tomtit & Thistle* (a trio of late 1890s Dearle designs). This success, augmented by an increased interest in tapestries and upholstered furniture, was to be a short-lived salvation for the brand and business.

ABOVE LEFT: A doctor said of William Morris' death 'the disease is simply having done more work than most ten men' He lies beneath a simple Philip Webb tombstone in St. George's Churchyard in Kelmscott, Oxfordshire. ABOVE: While Merton Abbey produced most Morris & Co. products, it was the sole responsibility of Jeffrey & Co. to print the wallpapers.

Royal patronage

In 1887 Queen Victoria commissioned
William Morris to design a wallpaper
incorporating her VRI Cipher for Balmoral
Castle. Some 24 years later in 1911, Morris
& Co. Decorators Ltd. was commissioned
to provide various items of furnishings and
Coronation thrones for King George V and
Queen Mary. Subsequently the company
was granted its first Royal Warrant, which
was proudly illuminated on all point-of-sale
literature and stationery.

Bower 100

BLOCK No. 002002 GROUND No. *Sold 27/ was W.O.*

20 REPEATS PER PCE.
PLATES COLS. WKGS.
// PRINTS //COLS. //WKGS.

Jeffrey & Co.

The VRI paper, like all the Morris & Co. wallpapers, was printed by Jeffery & Co., an Islington block printer renowned for its artistic sensitivity, that had produced Morris & Co. wallpapers since 1864. Two years later the highly talented and creative Metford Warner joined the firm. Under his direction Jeffery & Co. would rise to undreamed-of heights in the service of art and its application to the wallpaper industry.

On becoming sole proprietor in 1871, Warner employed on a freelance basis many well-known artist-designers of the time including William Burges, Walter Crane, Christopher Dresser, Lewis F. Day, Charles Eastlake, Kate Faulkner, E.W. Godwin, Owen Jones, Arthur Silver, C.F.A. Voysey and many others.

Warner's sons, Horace and Albert, worked as designers for Jeffery & Co. and became co-owners in 1898. The firm was incorporated in 1923 and Warner retired the following year. In 1926 the company was taken over by the Wall Paper Manufacturers Limited.

This was a monopoly, in combination controlling 98 per cent of all UK wallpaper manufacturing, which Sanderson's Chiswick factory had joined on its incorporation in 1899.

Jeffery & Co. papers were sold through Sanderson's Berners Street trade showrooms and in 1927, all distribution of Jeffery & Co. wallpapers was transferred to Sanderson while the factory log books, printing blocks and rollers were relocated to Sanderson's manufacturing unit at Chiswick. The following year there was a devastating fire at Chiswick and the Morris & Co. printing blocks, match pieces and colour records were relocated to Sanderson's prestigious new wallpaper mill at Perivale.

Wallpaper production was severely depleted for two years until the new mill was fully operational in 1930. The Perivale factory sustained production of Morris & Co. wallpapers until 1941 when it was turned over to the war effort, producing Red Cross tents, ammunition boxes and camouflage.

Plain wallpapers

Lack of manpower and raw materials during the First World War forced the closure of large parts of Merton Abbey, while by the end of 1917 the Oxford Street shop had relocated to the up-and-coming London vicinity of Hanover Square (17 George Street, which still bears an English Heritage Blue Plaque). The trend for unembellished interiors and a lack of pattern heralded the arrival of plain wallpapers which, by the mid 1920s, were *de rigueur*.

Desperate to meet the demand for plain walls and simple borders, Morris & Co. impetuously launched a collection of hand-stippled wallpapers in a vain attempt to fend off mass-market competition. These papers were sold by Morris & Co. at the exorbitant price of 16 shillings and three pence (16/3d) per piece (roll) whereas the Sanderson stained paper equivalent was a mere two shillings (2/-) per piece for a product with very little discernible difference.

THIS PAGE: (fabrics from right to left) 'Coiling Trail', an adapted Bannister Hall chintz block printed by Thomas Clarkson was one of the first three chintzes issued by Morris, Marshall, Faulkner & Co. in 1868, whilst 'Tangley' and 'Holkam' were both adapted 19th century textiles printed at Merton Abbey during the First World War. OPPOSITE: A small pattern book from the Hanover Square Showroom displaying hand stippled wallpapers together with 'Orange' and 'Lily' block printed borders and corners circa 1917.

MORRIS & COMPANY

Between the wars

In 1925 the company was once again re-organised and registered under the new name of Morris & Co. Art-workers Limited. However, the twin perils of an ageing artisan workforce and the difficulty of sourcing natural dyestuffs and raw materials led to a failure to maintain traditional work methods. This resulted in a mass-production mentality and unsatisfactory products such as machine-printed plain papers being sold during the 1930s. However, the ongoing commissions for block-printed wallpapers by Jeffrey & Co. maintained some credibility, further supported by the outsourcing of its block printed cretonnes and chintzes to Stead McAlpin in Carlisle subsequent to Merton Abbey closing its fabric block printing department.

On the death of John Henry Dearle in 1932 all artistic prowess was lost. The order book shrank and it became evident that the firm would not survive in a competitive market. On the 21st March 1940 it went into voluntary liquidation. The capricious nature of interior decoration, inconsistent merchandise and product unreliability were all contributing factors to its demise.

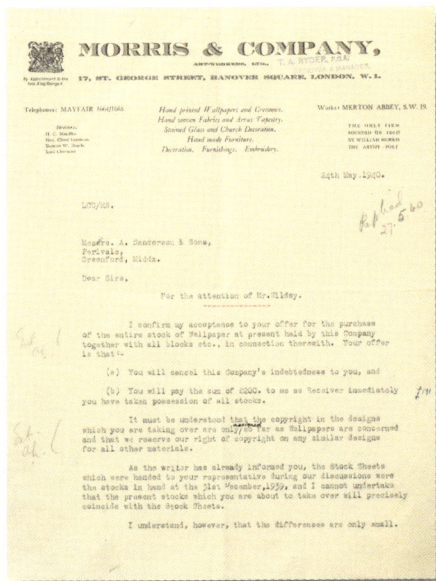

Sanderson buys Morris & Co.

Having taken over the Jeffrey & Co. wallpaper production in 1927, Arthur Sanderson & Sons Ltd. inherited exclusive rights to block-print all Morris & Co. wallpapers. This ongoing relationship made Sanderson the natural successor to Morris & Co. The Administrators approached Sanderson, who on the 24th May 1940 purchased Morris & Co. Art-workers Ltd. from the Receiver for the sum of £400.

The acquisition included the entire contents of the Hanover Square showroom including wallpaper and fabric samples, stand books and pattern books, together with the complete collection of wallpaper printing blocks, stock and exhaustive colour records. In addition to the priceless logbooks and hundreds of 'match pieces', there was also a comprehensive collection of Morris & Co. printed fabrics and original samples.

The purchase of the Morris & Co. business was completed during Great Britain's darkest hours, culminating in the evacuation of Dunkirk between 26th May and 4th June 1940.

The underlying logic behind the Sanderson family's acquisition of what was considered at the time to be a lifeless business will remain the subject of debate. Speculation suggests an opportunistic purchase rather than a strategic purchase, considering the financial handcuffs applied by the War Office to restrain commercial expenditure on anything other than the war effort.

One of the contributing factors to Sanderson's phenomenal growth was its expansion by acquisition of leading English wallpaper manufacturers, culminating in the acquired businesses being deprived of their identity and consumed by the voracious Sanderson brand. It could be assumed that the fate of Morris & Co. would follow in their wake – why promote a tarnished brand when your own is held in high esteem?

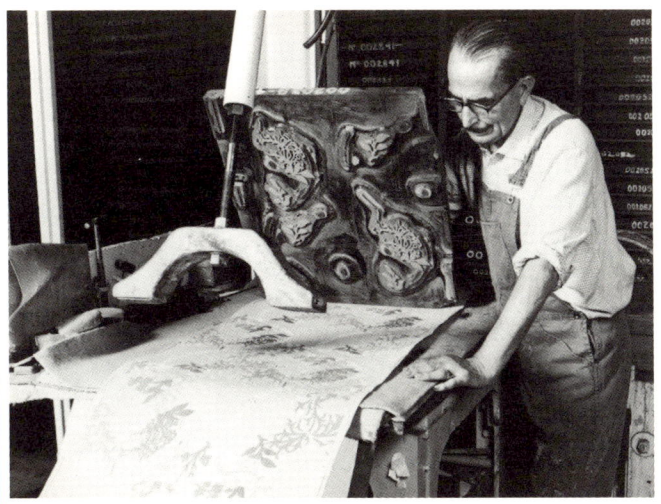

OAK TREE MORRIS & C°

Post Second World War

After the Second World War the revival of design and the decorative arts was a welcome relief from years of austerity. Whilst Scandinavian design was apparent before the war, it was to heavily influence interiors during the 1950s, with a predominance of pale colours, linear motifs, natural wood, rya rugs, freedom from clutter and a desire for cleanliness.

Although it took some years to return to normal production, in May 1945 the British wallpaper industry mounted a promotional exhibition in London's Pall Mall in association with the Central Institute of Art & Design. There were some 200 wallpaper displays and Sanderson, known for constantly creating, marketing and branding innovative wallpapers, was a major contributor. Surprisingly, the primary wallpaper listed in the catalogue was *The Acanthus* (William Morris, 1875). This was probably the first commercial showing by Sanderson of a Morris & Co. wallpaper design since purchasing the company.

In 1950 the Board of Trade gave Sanderson consent to introduce its first pattern books since 1941 which were proudly displayed at the 1951 Festival of Britain. With lacklustre post-war sales and the pressing need to market its brand and products, Sanderson launched a series of exhibitions at its Berners Street showroom to coincide with its new pattern books.

However, there was a noticeable absence of Morris & Co. block-printed wallpapers, as throughout this period most of Sanderson's wallpaper production was machine-printed, creating papers of great variety, style and price. Although the traditional craftsmanship of hand block printing was still practised, silk-screen printing, a relatively new hand made process, was gaining popularity at the top end of the market.

Subsequently, a pattern book was issued including surface-printed wallpapers which included the five original Morris & Co. machine-printed wallpapers first offered to the marketplace in the early 1900s. This gave consumers a limited selection of Morris & Co. designs at affordable prices, being five times cheaper than the hand-block equivalent.

47

Morris & the Psychedelic Sixties

Despite their being unfashionable at the time, Sanderson continued to print and market 'ageing' Morris & Co. wallpapers in order to keep the block-printers busy. In 1960, to celebrate the Sanderson centenary, Perivale, Sanderson's wallpaper printing factory, issued several major collections, including one book with a modicum of Morris & Co. block-printed wallpapers, re-coloured by the Sanderson studio in hues of orange, purple, lemon and pink to be more in vogue and reflecting a cacophony of colour.

The decade plundered the past for inspiration resulting in a hotchpotch of styles, which were not replicated but given an irreverent makeover of their own. Bright colours and flamboyant designs were part of the groovy scene yet, on opening an innocent-looking Sanderson wallpaper pattern book, psychedelic Morris & Co. images leapt from the page, with colourations to 'blow your mind'. Regrettably, such wallpapers did not appeal to the Swinging Sixties trendsetters in their pads on the King's Road and Carnaby Street.

In celebration of its centenary in 1960, Sanderson launched a book of Morris & Co. block printed wallpapers containing designs re-coloured in palettes thought to be more relevant to the time, causing much discontent within the Morris fraternity.
THIS PAGE: (clockwise from top left) 'Chrysanthemum', 'Bachelor's Button', 'Sunflower' and 'Indian'.
OPPOSITE: 'Granville' was designed by Dearle in 1896 as a block printed wallpaper and subsequently adapted by Sanderson during the late 1960s into a linen union printed fabric in flamboyant colours.

Morris & Co. fabrics reborn

Although the Morris & Co. designs were the reserve of the Perivale Wallpaper Studio, it was Sanderson's newly appointed fabric design manager who had the foresight to capitalise on William Morris' Arts & Crafts heredity. During the early 1960s George Lowe migrated south from Lightbown Aspinall, the Wall Paper Manufacturers Ltd. branch in Stockport, to Sanderson's Fabric Print Works at Uxbridge. Subsequently, instigated by Lowe, Sanderson issued its first comprehensive collection of flatbed screen-printed Morris & Co. fabrics to partner the existing wallpaper collection. This key development not only capitalised on a fashionable decorating trend but also earned the approbation of Lowe's close friend and neighbour, John Morris, a descendant of William Morris.

Contained within this fabric collection were *Brother Rabbit* (Morris 1882), *Willow Bough* (Morris 1887 & 1895) and *Eden* (Dearle 1905), printed by Stead McAlpin. But, more importantly, Lowe introduced five 'new' Morris & Co. printed fabrics into the collection – *Vine* (Morris 1874), *Marigold* (Morris 1875), *Chrysanthemum* (Morris 1877), *Bachelors Button* (Morris 1892) and *Golden Lily* (Dearle 1899), adapted and rescaled to 48 inches wide from the original 21 inch wide wallpaper blocks.

Probably considered relatively insignificant at the time, the creation of these five new Morris & Co. printed fabrics proved to be the strategic cornerstone in re-establishing the Morris & Co. brand. It also endorsed the Sanderson print works as host to a new generation of Morris & Co. fabrics, notably the celebrated *Chrysanthemum* and glorious *Golden Lily*, both successful at the time and remain in the collection today.

THIS PAGE: 'Bachelor's Button' designed by William Morris as a wallpaper in 1892 was subsequently re-coloured by Sanderson and block printed in colours thought to be more relevant to the 1960s. THIS PAGE, INSET: Simultaneously, Sanderson Fabrics launched an adapted version of 'Bachelor's Button' printed on linen union and featured on the front cover of VISTA, the Sanderson house magazine. OPPOSITE & INSET: 'Chrysanthemum', designed by William Morris in 1877, was one of five Morris & Co. block printed wallpapers adapted to fabric in the early 1960s. 'Chrysanthemum' also appeared in this Sanderson 'Our Man' advert.

SANDERSON

VISTA

Number Five

A periodical look into the Sanderson world of furnishing fabrics

Spring 1964

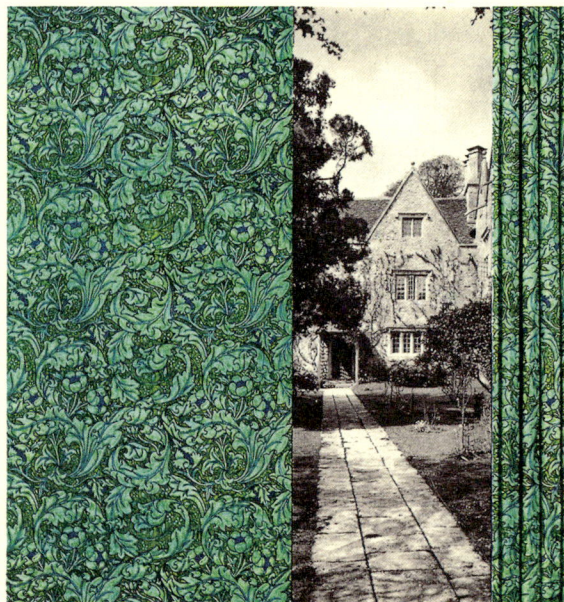

OUR MA
WILLIA

Our Man is prou
his Morris wallp
Sweden to Sas
complimented o
Morris revival.
modesty that M
and that Sanders
to give his desig

The Morris Collection by Sanderson

The early 1960s saw the Sanderson Perivale wallpaper business and the Sanderson Uxbridge fabric business simultaneously re-launch independent Morris & Co. wallpaper and fabric books entitled '*The Morris Collection by Sanderson*'. The first adapted Morris & Co. wallpaper design, *Bachelors Button*, was printed at Uxbridge and given pride of place on the front cover of *Vista*, the Sanderson house magazine.

The post-war period saw a resurgence of interest in the Morris style, propagated by the introduction of sensational printed textile designs such as *Golden Lily* (adapted from John Henry Dearle's 1899 wallpaper design) aimed specifically at the Sixties' 'dedicated followers of fashion' (The Kinks' 1966 hit single). Meanwhile, the Sanderson 'Our Man' adverts, occasionally illustrating Morris & Co. imagery, attempted to revitalise consumer interest in patterned wallpapers by extolling the virtues of quality, design and colour.

By the late 1960s the revival of William Morris and Victoriana in general was impacting not only on the commercial world but also on the academic fraternity. Sanderson's logical next step was to advertise its Morris & Co. designs in The William Morris Society journals and, for its part, the society was more than happy to endorse subsequent collections of block-printed Morris & Co. wallpapers, albeit some contained re-coloured patterns in deep purple and sky blue.

With Morris & Co. patterns and colourways on the loose and unchecked, even the Berners Street showroom staff could be seen wearing outfits in Morris' designs whilst presenting somewhat *risqué* Morris & Co. room sets to potential clients.

'ALKS ORRIS

eat success of fabrics. From n, he's been ibution to the s with proper a great artist r it a privilege culation.

Our Man owns all Morris's original wallpaper blocks in perfect condition. He's struck out on his own, too—devising modern colour ways which go perfectly with Morris's individual genius. Each paper in the Morris collection is hand-printed in a solid depth of colour which no other process can equal. The range of Morris's designs runs all the way from grandeur to delicacy. Odds are you have a room which a Morris paper or fabric could transform. Why not come to the Sanderson showrooms and see for yourself?

SANDERSON WALLPAPERS AND FABRICS

Showrooms: *Berners Street, London, W.1. and in Glasgow, Edinburgh, Leeds, Manchester, Liverpool, Birmingham, Leicester, Exeter, Bristol, Southampton, Brighton, Newcastle, Cardiff.*

wpm

THIS PAGE: 'Golden Lily' was first designed as a block printed wallpaper in 1899 by John Henry Dearle and reinterpreted into a fabric by Sanderson during the early 1960s. THIS PAGE, INSET: The first Triad Collection launched in 1962 comprised matching wallpaper and fabric together with a companion paper. By 1976 this Triad Collection dominated the UK furnishing market being the ultimate source for co-ordination which, of course, included commercialised adaptations of Morris & Co. block prints. OPPOSITE: 'Blackthorn', designed for wallpaper by John Henry Dearle in 1892, reflects a similar layout to Morris' 'Honeysuckle' fabric of 1876 and is often incorrectly attributed to William Morris. 'Blackthorn' first appeared as a fabric in a 1975 Sanderson collection and is still available today. OPPOSITE, INSET: William Morris created the original design for 'Myrtle' in 1875; even so the pattern was not issued as a block printed wallpaper until three years after his death. The original received an irreverent makeover in the form of this matching gravure printed wallpaper and screen printed fabric seen here in the 1976 Triad Collection.

52

Morris & Co. fabrics in the 1970s

In the early 1970s, rising labour and manufacturing costs at the Perivale site necessitated a more fluid approach to demands for Morris & Co. block-printed wallpapers whereby special commissions and bespoke colourations were undertaken to offset the enormous factory overheads.

With sales of block-printed Morris & Co. wallpapers faltering, the Morris & Co. fabrics were gaining momentum in the wake of a second collection launched in 1975. This collection was acknowledged to be one of Sanderson's most profitable, with designs being sold extensively throughout the UK furniture industry. The most popular was *Golden Lily*, which at its peak achieved sales in excess of 5,000 metres a month. In the same year, the ever-popular Triad Collection of co-ordinated wallpapers and fabrics presented four Morris & Co. designs, *Rose* (Morris 1877), *Christchurch* (Morris 1883), *Blackthorn* (Dearle 1892) and *Myrtle* (Morris first printed 1899).

By the late 1970s both hand-block and screen-printed Perivale wallpapers were suffering from declining sales. In desperation, another hand-block Heritage Collection of wallpapers was launched. Its eminent designs by Owen Jones, William Morris and C.F.A. Voysey ran contrary to the futuristic, contemporary patterns that made up the major tranche of the collection – a certain cocktail for failure. This was further aggravated by the inclusion of incompatible 'exhilarating' new Morris & Co. colourways, far removed from the Morris ethos, which caused much distress among William Morris aficionados.

The re-emergence of the Morris & Co. brand

The 1980s saw many changes at Sanderson but, perhaps the most significant was the arrival of A.L. ('Lee') Taylor as chief executive in 1982. Up to this point, Sanderson Wallcoverings and Sanderson Fabrics had traded as separate entities, united by name alone. Collectively the businesses lacked direction and clarity; rationalisation and restructuring were essential. The outcome was that divisions merged, with resources, sales forces and design studios combined.

Sanderson's strategy was redirected from manufacturing to marketing and its brand was re-established by creating and merchandising cohesive collections to serve the decorative market rather than being all things to all men. However, the decision to resurrect the Morris & Co. brand was held in abeyance.

Taylor was instrumental in vehemently invigorating the Design Studio and in 1982 Michael Parry (previously merchandise manager) was appointed design manager pending George Lowe's retirement. A new purpose-built archive was established at Uxbridge, which evolved into a resource for the design and marketing teams. Giving due consideration to brand clarity, it was decided to issue the first branded Morris & Co. block-printed wallpaper collection since Sanderson had purchased the company some 45 years earlier.

Concurrently, Parry was given approval to transfer a selection of block-printed Morris & Co. wallpaper patterns on to surface roller printing machines, with a view to marketing a more affordable and easier-to-use product. The results were impressive and almost indistinguishable from the originals in appearance and finish due to the improved printing techniques since William Morris' time.

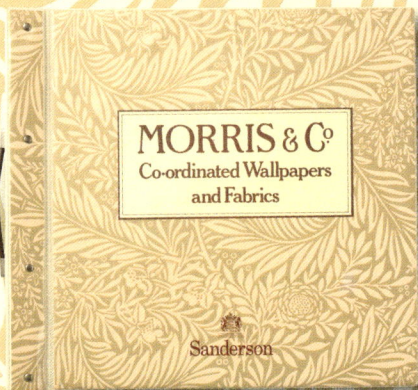

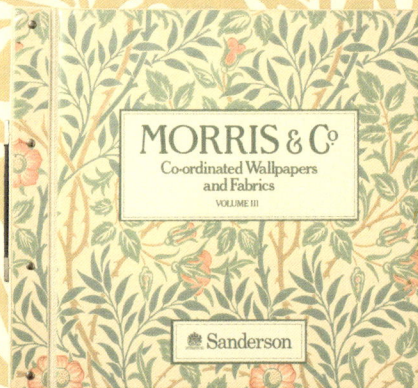

TOP: The first Morris & Co. book of machine printed wallpapers and fabrics was launched in 1984 and featured 'Larkspur' (designed by William Morris as a block printed wallpaper in 1872) on the cover. ABOVE: The third collection issued in 1988 with 'Sweet Briar' (designed by John Henry Dearle in 1912) on the cover pushed the boundaries of multi-colour surface printing technology. BACKGROUND: 'Larkspur' surface printed wallpaper.

THIS PAGE: 'Acorn' designed by William Morris in 1879, featured in the 1988 Morris & Co. Co-ordinated Wallpaper and Fabric Collection. This machine printed wallpaper, to some indistinguishable from its block printed parent, remains in the collection today due to its popularity in the USA. Such wallpapers have proved to be extremely successful, being more affordable while maintaining the quality and integrity of the original block prints.

THIS PAGE &
OPPOSITE: 'Willow Bough',
designed by William Morris
in 1887, is perhaps the most
recognisable of all Morris &
Co. designs and was licensed
by Sanderson to WestPoint
Pepperell in 1987. Then
the second largest sheeting
producer in the United States,
WestPoint created this 'Willow
Bough' Classic Master
Bedroom Ensemble for which
they received a prestigious
design award.

The enduring designs of Morris & Co.

The first Morris & Co. machine-printed, co-ordinated wallpaper and fabric collection was launched in 1984, with the papers expertly printed by Fiona Wallpapers in Faaborg in Denmark. At Michael Parry's request the machines were slowed down to simulate the character of the Morris & Co. block prints. The inaugural collection was premiered at Sanderson's Berners Street showroom in the new, purpose-built 'Morris Room'.

The initiative to produce machine-printed Morris & Co. wallpapers proved extremely successful and necessitated follow-up collections. Nobody guessed, however, that this move would ultimately re-establish Morris & Co. not only as a brand, but also as a business.

The versatility and lasting qualities of Morris & Co. designs are best illustrated by *Willow Bough* (designed by William Morris in 1887 and subsequently adapted by him for a cretonne and printed at Merton Abbey in 1895). By far the most popular of all the Morris & Co. designs, it has never been out of production, being available as a block-printed wallpaper, a printed textile, a printed sheer, jacquard upholstery cloth, a tapestry, gift items and bed linen. *Willow Bough* was therefore the obvious design to be adapted to surface-printed wallpaper and first appeared as such in the 1990 Morris & Co. co-ordinated collection.

Morris & Co. – A separate company once more

Following a strategic review of the entire Sanderson business, the emphasis of the company changed, re-establishing the authenticity of both the Sanderson and Morris & Co. brands by liberating them from the mire of the mass market and concentrating on the decorative arena. As a consequence, in 1989, the Morris & Co. brand was extricated from beneath the Sanderson umbrella and marketed in its own right.

A 1991 survey carried out on Sanderson's behalf to assess unprompted brand recognition of wallpaper and fabric businesses within the UK, revealed Sanderson as the market leader, closely followed by Marks & Spencer, John Lewis, Morris & Co. and Liberty. The outcome of this survey revealed unparalleled recognition for both brands and galvanised Sanderson into marketing the Morris & Co. brand and corporate identity in absolution, vindicating 50 years of isolation from public gaze.

Although Sanderson's Perivale factory closed in 1972, the tiny artisan block-printing studio remained until the late 1980s. On retiring, the block printers trained a new team at the recently acquired factory in Lancashire. With continuity assured, a second collection of hand block printed Morris & Co. wallpapers was issued in 1990 taking pride of place in

the Morris Room at the Berners Street showroom. Random Morris & Co. designs sporadically appeared in Sanderson collections, nevertheless, in 1995 *Willow Bough* and other solitary Morris & Co. patterns made their final curtain call on the Sanderson stage. By the end of the 1990s the independent brand strategies for both Morris & Co. and Sanderson were well established.

In August 2003, Walker Greenbank PLC, headed by John Sach, purchased Sanderson together with Morris & Co. and embarked on a massive investment programme to replenish stocks, re-sample the UK and export markets and, more importantly, bankroll new collections for both brands supported by significant advertising campaigns. Subsequent to the purchase, Walker Greenbank transferred all Sanderson and Morris & Co. production to their own mills, namely wallpapers to Anstey and printed fabrics to Standfast & Barracks.

The initial inroads into export, pioneered by Morris, laid the foundations for what is today a significant international business trading in major markets worldwide, in particular, the United States, Australasia, Japanese and Russian markets, which were augmented by the dominant UK market allied to important royalty income from licensees worldwide.

OPPOSITE: Weaves from the Pimpernel Collection included 'Planet', 'Artichoke' and 'Larkspur', released in 2008. OPPOSITE, INSET LEFT: The second Morris & Co. block printed wallpaper pattern book issued in 1990 premièring the newly created Morris & Co., corporate identity sustained and maintained to this day. OPPOSITE, INSET RIGHT: Morris & Co. Volume V pattern book released in 2008.

THIS PAGE: The advertising image used for Morris & Co. Volume V in 2008 showing 'Thistle', originally designed by John Henry Dearle in 1897, and being one of only five surface roller machine printed wallpapers pioneered by Morris & Co.

RIGHT: William Morris' four poster bed curtains at Kelmscott Manor were embroidered by May Morris in 1891 with the assistance of Lily Yates and Ellen Wright. This was the inspiration for the resplendent 'Kelmscott Tree' embroidery from The Archive Collections of 2011.

An enduring brand image

The remarkable development, ascendance, resilience, reputation and influence of the Morris & Co. brand derives from the ingenuity, creativity and craftsmanship of William Morris and his colleagues. This enduring legacy continues to inspire, reassured by a commitment not to reinvent this iconic brand. No other interior company has remained so true to its heritage.

Today, the insatiable demand for undiscovered Morris & Co. patterns has paved the way for the Design Team to create inspirational adaptations of original Morris & Co. imagery be it stained glass, tapestries or documents contained within the Morris & Co. Archive. Yet convincingly, one is assured by the authority and everlasting permanence of these rejuvenated Morris & Co. images.

The underlying strength of these vintage patterns is not only their timelessness but also their ability to evolve into innovative renditions relevant to current fashion. Today Morris & Co. wallpapers and fabrics have international appeal whether decorating Victorian cottages or New York apartments. Newly interpreted Morris & Co. collections have enduring qualities that stand the test of time.

THIS PAGE: Embroidery was one of the mainstays of the Morris & Co. business and during the late 1880s John Henry Dearle designed numerous embroidery patterns similar to 'Mary Isobel', seen here on a four-fold screen together with an occasional chair covered in 'Orchard' inspired by medieval tapestries woven at Merton Abbey. Both 'Mary Isobel' and 'Orchard' are from The Archive Collections of 2011.

This room set from The Archive Collections of 2011 features 'Acanthus' tapestry on the Chesterfield, one of Morris' most iconic wallpaper patterns first registered in 1875; 'Branch' cut velvet, taken from the 1871 Morris & Co. block print wallpaper on the chair together with 'Bluebell' printed curtains inspired by Morris' 1876 block printed cotton.

150th Anniversary of Morris & Co

In celebration of the 150th anniversary of Morris, Marshall, Faulkner & Company, an inspirational collection of tapestries, velvets, embroideries, wallpapers and printed fabrics was launched in 2011.

"These newly interpreted designs use modern production techniques to produce fabrics and wallpapers closer to the originals than ever before. The embroideries include two adapted from those in Morris' bedroom at Kelmscott Manor and of the seven weaves, two have been woven in wool as the originals. Others are adapted from wallpaper designs and have been woven as tapestries, velvets and damasks.

The depth of colour and definition of the hand block printed wallpapers has been reproduced using a combination of surface and flexo printing techniques. Multi-coloured designs such as Golden Lily and Pimpernel are almost indistinguishable from the originals with a richness of colour and authenticity not previously possible with machine printing.

Bringing old Morris & Co. designs back to the marketplace is always a pleasure and his unique design philosophy seems as relevant today as ever. New production techniques now make these originally hand crafted designs affordable – just as William Morris always hoped they would be" – Liz Cann, Design Director.

63

64

with thanks to:

Art Gallery of South Australia
Birmingham Museums & Art Gallery
Cheltenham Art Gallery & Museum
Fine Art Society
Kelmscott Manor
Society of Antiquaries of London
The National Trust
Victoria & Albert Museum
Wightwick Manor
William Morris Gallery
William Morris Society
Victoria Blair, Liz Cann,
Annabel Freyberg, Hugo Ripley,
Selina Carbutt, David Smallridge
and David Walker.

PHOTOGRAPHY CREDITS

All Saints Church, Selsley *Page 9*
Art Gallery of South Australia *Pages 8-9*
Chris Everard *Front end page, pages 12, 13, 27, 35, 59, 61, 62, 63, 64*
Corbis: *Pages 6 (inset right), 7 (inset left), 29 (insets top & bottom)*
Gary O'Kane *Page 60, back end pages*
Getty *Pages 4 (inset), 14 (inset), 30 (inset top & bottom), 31 (insets top & bottom), 37 (inset bottom)*
Liam Jones *Pages 1, 6, 7, 10, 11, 14, 15, 16, 17, 20, 21, 22, 30-31 (background), 33, 36-37 (background), 38, 39, 40, 41, 42, 43, 44, 45, 46, 47, 48, 49, 50 (background), 51 (background), 52 (background & inset), 53 (background & inset), 54 (background & inset), 57, 58 (insets top & bottom), 65*
Marica McEwan *Pages 28-29 (background)*
National Portrait Gallery *Pages 6 (inset centre), 7 (insets centre & right), 37 (inset top)*
Sanderson Archive *Pages 47 (inset), 50 (inset), 51 (inset), 55, 56*
Tobias Harvey *Pages 26, 34, 58 (background)*
V&A Images, Victoria & Albert Museum *Page 24*
William Morris Gallery *Cover, front end pages, pages 2-3, 6 (inset left), 18, 19, 22-23 (background & inset), 25, 28, 32*
William Morris Society *Pages 4-5*

PLACES & ORGANISATIONS OF INTEREST

Birmingham Museums & Art Gallery
Chamberlain Square, Birmingham,
West Midlands B3 3DH
0121 303 2834 www.bmag.org.uk

Blackwell, The Arts & Crafts House
Cumbria LA23 3JT
015394 46139 www.blackwell.org.uk

Carlyle's House
24 Cheyne Row, Chelsea, London SW3 5HL
020 7352 7087
www.nationaltrust.org.uk/carlyleshouse

Cragside
Rothbury, Morpeth, Northumberland, NE65 7PX
01669 620333
www.nationaltrust.org.uk/cragside

Kelmscott Manor
Kelmscott, Lechlade,
Gloucestershire, GL7 3HJ
01367 252486 www.kelmscottmanor.co.uk

Linley Sambourne House
18 Stafford Terrace, London W8 7BH
020 7602 3316
www.rbkc.gov.uk/linleysambournehouse

Red House
Red House Lane, Bexleyheath,
London DA6 8JF
020 8304 9878
www.nationaltrust.org.uk/redhouse

Society for the Protection of Ancient Buildings
37 Spital Square, London E1 6DY
020 7377 1644 www.spab.org.uk

Standen
West Hoathly Road, East Grinstead,
West Sussex, RH19 4NE
01342 323029
www.nationaltrust.org.uk/standen

Victoria & Albert Museum
Cromwell Road, South Kensington,
London SW7 2RL
020 7942 2000 www.vam.ac.uk

The Whitworth Art Gallery
Oxford Road, Manchester, MI5 6ER
0161 275 7450
www.whitworth.manchester.ac.uk

Wightwick Manor
Wightwick Bank, Wolverhampton,
West Midlands, WV6 8EE
01902 761400
www.nationaltrust.org.uk/wightwickmanor

William Morris Gallery
Lloyd Park Water House, Lloyd Park,
Forest Road, Walthamstow, London E17 4PP
020 8496 4390
www.walthamforest.gov.uk/william-morris

William Morris Society
Kelmscott House Museum, 26 Upper Mall,
Hammersmith, London W6 9TA
020 8741 3735
www.morrissociety.org

AN INTRODUCTORY READING LIST

EP Thompson *William Morris, Romantic to Revolutionary,* 1955

J.W.Mackail *The Life of William Morris,* Two Volumes 1899

Peter Faulkner *William Morris – The Critical Heritage*, 1973

P. Floud *The Wallpaper Designs of William Morris* Penrose Annual LIV, 1960

A. Briggs (ed) *William Morris: Selected Writings and Designs,* 1962

P. Faulkner *Against the Age: An Introduction to William Morris,* 1980

L. Parry *William Morris Textiles,* 1983

G. Naylor *William Morris by Himself,* 1988

C. Harvey & J Press *William Morris: Design and Enterprise in Victorian Britain,* 1991

F. MacCarthy *William Morris: A Life For Our Time,* 1994

L. Parry (ed), *William Morris,* V&A Catalogue, 1996

Mary Schoeser, *Sanderson: The Essence of English Decoration,* 2010

MORRIS & C°

UK HEAD OFFICE
Chalfont House, Oxford Road
Denham UB9 4DX UK
Tel: 0844 543 9500
Fax: 0844 543 9555
Email: enquiries@william-morris.co.uk

LONDON SHOWROOM
Design Centre Chelsea Harbour
Lots Road, London SW10 0XE UK
Tel: 0844 543 4749
Fax: +44 (0)207 351 9677
Email: enquiries@william-morris.co.uk

CONTRACTS DEPARTMENT
Chalfont House, Oxford Road
Denham. UB9 4DX UK
Tel: +44 (0)845 123 6810
Fax: +44 (0)845 123 6811
Email: denham@walkergreenbankcontracts.com
Web: www.walkergreenbankcontracts.com

FRENCH OFFICE/SHOWROOM
19 Rue de Mail
75002 Paris, France
Tel: +33 1 4041 1770
Fax: +33 1 4041 1771
Email: serviceclient@sandersonfrance.fr

USA HEAD OFFICE
800 Huyler Street, Teterboro,
NJ 07608, USA
Tel: +1 201 399 0500
Fax: +1 201 399 0501
Email: customerservices@a-sanderson.co.uk

NEW YORK SHOWROOM
Suite 409, D&D Building
979 Third Avenue
New York, NY 10022 USA
Tel: +1 212 319 7220
Fax: +1 212 593 6184
Email: customerservices@a-sanderson.co.uk

www.william-morris.co.uk

"If I were asked to say what is at once the most important production of Art and the